The P

Self-Identity

Confidence. Boundaries. Self-Acceptance.

. . .

Destiny S. Harris

<u>Enjoy A Free Gift At The End Of This Book</u>

Table of Contents

The Power of Self-Identity   1

Article 1   8

Article 2   16

Article 3   21

Article 4   30

Article 5   39

Article 6   48

Article 7   58

The End   70

Thank You Note   72

About Destiny S. Harris   73

Connect W/ Destiny S. Harris   75

Leave A Review   76

Share This Read   77

When You're Feeling Series   78

Overcoming BS Series   80

Mental Rescue Series   81

Self-Care Affirmations Series   82

Good Day, Good Night Series   83

Boost Your Self-Esteem Series   84

The Law of Attraction Series   85

Level 1: Finance Series   86

Building Wealth Series   87

Post-Incarceration Series   88

Free Gift   89

The Power of

Self-Identity

Confidence. Boundaries. Self-Acceptance.

Article 1

Nip It In The Bud

When it comes to neglect, you have a limited amount of time before the effects become apparent in your life.

The continuation of unproductive patterns in your behavior, choices, and thinking is **easy**; this is why neglect is *common.* Another precarious plight that develops from neglect is that you don't always **realize** the neglect's ramifications (in whatever areas of your life it applies). *The insidious effects of progressing without pausing for change can devastate one's life.*

How many people and things have you neglected?

When one neglects their health—naturally, the body eventually responds with disease and ailments.

When one neglects their relationships—naturally, the other party becomes cold and/or the relationship suffers, and closeness is removed from the equation.

When one neglects their career—naturally, they stagnate and work the remainder of their lives for mediocre pay, mediocre companies, and mediocre opportunities.

When one neglects their mental health—naturally, the mind becomes a monster out of control that makes it hard to come back from.

When one neglects their diet and nutrition—naturally, they tend to gain weight or set their bodies up for invitations to various kinds of sickness and inconveniences.

When one neglects their personal growth—naturally, they tend to avoid progress in life, living in mediocrity—barely tapping into their limitless potential.

When one neglects their finances—naturally, they invite debt, hardship, and unnecessary stress and inconvenience into their lives.

When one neglects consistently working on their goals—naturally, they will never reach them, or the time it takes to reach their goals will drastically increase—prolonging success.

Whatever your habits are will have consequences. What you put into the world, you get back. What actions, habits, and thinking patterns you settle for daily will find their ways back to you.

Today's Challenge: Think about all of your habits, behaviors, and thinking patterns; which ones will have short-term and/or long-term negative consequences? Nip these in the bud **today**.

Question

What am I neglecting?

_____

_____

_____

_____

_____

Notes Section

Article 2

Sit on It

When you are struggling to make a decision, learn to <u>sit on it</u>. It's not always a bad thing to procrastinate on making a decision—especially when the decision is a life-altering one.

When you don't know what to do, sit still. As time passes, your answer will come. You only need to be patient and keep making progress in the meantime. Be comfortable with putting things off, sitting still, and being patient. Be comfortable with making decisions <u>slowly</u>.

Time away from decision-making will provide more clarity when the time is right.

Question

What decisions do I need to sit still on for now?

_____

_____

_____

_____

_____

Notes Section

Article 3

5 Reasons Why We Willingly Choose Mediocrity

Mediocrity is its own pandemic. It's easy to settle. It's easy to stay the same. It's easy to continue doing what you've always done. It's easy to accept whatever you're given and whatever comes your way. It's easy to choose mediocrity willingly, and here are five reasons why.

1. Habits

Our habits are what determine what kind of life we will have. Our habits have the power to affect us in multiple aspects of our lives. Most people choose mediocrity because of their habits. Habits are like addictions, and it can be a challenge to stop any habit cold turkey unless you have a prevailing motivation to do so.

2. Self-Worth

The second reason why people choose mediocrity derives from a lack of self-worth. If you ever see someone that willingly accepts mistreatment or disrespect when they are **paying** for service, or someone willingly stays in an abusive relationship, it's because they lack self-worth.

Until a person establishes a healthy sense of self-worth, they will continue to live a mediocre life, they will continue to have mediocre opportunities, they will continue to experience mediocre relationships, and they will continue to accept mediocre or worse treatment from others.

3. Comfort Zone

The third reason people choose to live mediocre lives is that **it's easy.** It's easier to accept:

- Mistreatment
- Average opportunities
- Unhealthy relationships

- Poor habits
- And mediocrity

Because it requires **ZERO** effort. You have to invest time, energy, thought, and willpower to *not* accept mediocrity. You have to be willing to be uncomfortable for a temporary amount of time so that you can be comfortable indefinitely.

4. Boundaries

The fourth reason people settle for mediocrity is a lack of boundaries. When you don't have boundaries, you tend to settle for whatever comes your way. When boundaries are absent from a person's life, they are like a house with no fence—anyone and anything can get in and do what they want. A person without boundaries willingly accepts mediocrity because they don't have the gumption to live any differently.

5. Exposure

The more you expose yourself, the more your mind expands; this is why it is critical to travel, explore new spaces, continually learn, and continually explore new people, environments, and experiences. The more exposed you are, the more you will question life, limits, boundaries, habits, relationships, your self-worth, and the way you live life. The more exposure you have, the more your confidence grows, and the less you accept mediocrity willingly. I'm sure everyone has experienced the thought of, "I wish I knew then, what I know now."

In conclusion, the five reasons why people willingly choose mediocrity is because of their habits, lack of self-worth, it's comfortable staying in your comfort zone, it's difficult to enforce and establish boundaries—especially later in life, and a lack of exposure.

Going Forward: Will you choose to *willingly* accept mediocrity or will you get out of your usual and try something different, so your life can change for the better? *Take the leap, you won't regret it.*

Question

Am I choosing average?

Notes Section

Article 4

Forgetting Who You Are

3 Key Areas Where Loss of Identity Is Common

There are times we forget who we are, how much strength and resilience we have, and what our values are. Some people are lucky enough to have people around to help remind them that they are losing themselves. **But we always have one person we can rely on 100%, and that is ourselves.**

Hardship

Turbulent times can take their toll on us. If we aren't careful, we fail to remember how much strength lies within us. It's easy to forget how resilient you are when you keep getting pounded with unfortunate circumstances, which is why you have to constantly train and fuel your spirit, soul, and mind. Everyone has strength and willpower within them; you only have to dig it out. Prepare for hardship in the "good and easy times," so you will always be ready for testing times.

How do you prepare for hardship? Here are a few ideas:

- Read personal development books.
- Help others through their times of hardship.
- Learn about stoicism.
- Maintain self-discipline in all areas of your life.
- Take charge of your emotions; don't let them guide your life.

Relationships

Relationships do one of two things: they elevate, or they hinder. Some entanglements become claustrophobic to the point where you lose your entire identity—and forget who you are.

In the infatuation (usually the beginning) phase of a relationship, it's effortless to become so encapsulated that you lose yourself, your values, your boundaries, and your focus. Many people get past this initial phase of a relationship, but others don't. I'm sure you've met couples that seem inseparable; they do *everything* together, and you usually never see them doing things alone. This indicates that identities have been lost or combined into one identity, which has its own consequences (e.g., bitterness, boredom, unhappiness, depression, regret, etc.) later in life.

A way to recover your identity in a relationship is to start implementing boundaries **immediately** with your time, goals, and interests. Don't give up pieces of your identity for anyone; once you start, it's more challenging to stop.

Work

For many, career is **everything** (and I'm not talking about the people who are genuinely passionate about their work—that's different). It's easy to tell these people apart; these people easily get stressed about work, only talk about work, spend their weekends looking at work, and are always in the work slack or other chat/communication channels. People who have lost their identities to their career don't have hobbies outside of work, nor do they have boundaries for their work.

The first step to regaining your identity—outside of work—is to set boundaries. The second step is to engage in other hobbies. The third step is to connect or reconnect with loved ones and friends. Too often, people overinvest in their jobs only to have them ripped away when they least expect it. *Jobs are temporary—remember this.*

In conclusion, we can lose our identities at any given point. To avoid an identity crisis, keep self-awareness close. Stay in tune with your surroundings, relationships, priorities, desires, and feelings. Remind yourself of who you are— even when you don't feel like you know. Believe that who you are is important enough to showcase to the world. Maintain and enforce firm boundaries with yourself and others. Finally, always remember to love yourself unconditionally and never sacrifice who you are for anyone or anything.

Question

How may I have forgotten who I am?

_____

_____

_____

_____

_____

Notes Section

Article 5

Release More Endorphins

They Feel Good & Make You Smile, So Why Not Release More?

Endorphins & Mental Health

Whenever my dogs play, go outside, go for a walk, or do anything physical, afterward, they're **ALL** smiles.

Do you know why? Because endorphins make you SMILE, feel good, enhance your mental health, and also help decrease the pain you might be experiencing in·your life mentally, physically, emotionally, and spiritually.

The world could be a little bit happier, a little bit more smiley, and feel a little bit more cheerful inside if they released more endorphins every day.

With depression and mental illness growing rampant, releasing endorphins is one **sure** way you can help combat negative feelings, states of beings, and moods. It does take some effort on your part, but you **always** feel better once you complete an endorphin-releasing activity.

Smile More & Be Grateful

We shouldn't be freaked out by people who often smile; instead, we should ask them what they have to smile about. Next, we should ask ourselves:

1. What can I smile about?
2. What can I be grateful for?
3. What do I **get** to do today that I might be taking for granted?

Being grateful can be transformative to your mental health.

Endorphin Releasing Ideas

Here are some easy ways to release endorphins:

- Dance to some catchy a** music.

- Complete a goal.

- Take a walk *first* thing in the morning.

- *Laugh* (very underrated).

- Workout with a friend.

- Stretch and focus on your breathing.

- Have a stimulating conversation.

- Complete an easter egg hunt.

- Go ziplining.

- Play ball with your dogs (one of my dogs is OBSESSED w/ playing fetch 24/7).

The way to release endorphins doesn't have to be in the form of a traditional workout. Get creative. Do something **fun**. Stimulate your mind, body, and soul. Try something you've never experienced before.

Walking

One of my favorite ways to release endorphins, help with any pain I feel in my body at times, and de-stress is to walk. The more I walk, the better I feel—holistically. When I consistently take walks, I notice multiple areas (e.g., work, mood, spiritual health, and mental clarity, to name a few.) of my life improve. Walking is also one of the *easiest* ways to feel better—immediately.

There are so many benefits of walking:

- Increase in mental clarity
- De-stress
- Gather new ideas
- De-escalate anger and anxiety
- Increase mobility
- Maintain a healthy weight

Closing Thoughts

Remember to laugh. Remember to smile. Remember to release *more* endorphins.

Life can take its toll on you when you forget to enjoy it. Your body, spirit, and overall health will thank you for consistently releasing more endorphins.

Take Action: What can you start doing more of to release endorphins starting today?

Question

How can I release more endorphins today?

_____

_____

_____

_____

_____

Notes Section

Article 6

Why Do We Reject Ourselves Prematurely?

Self-Sabotage

I'm sure we've all been guilty of self-sabotage at some point in our lives—some more than others. But why? What do we get out of rejecting ourselves before giving others, opportunities, and life a chance to show us that we are worthy of acceptance?

It's apparent that most of us want to be accepted, loved, praised, worthy, and respected in today's world. But before we can genuinely experience this from the world around us, *we* need to give **ourselves** acceptance, love, praise, self-worth, and respect; acceptance won't mean a thing coming from others if we don't even have the capacity to give it to ourselves.

The greatest trap in our life, is not success, popularity or power, but self-rejection.—Henry Nouwen

Self-Worth

The foundation of self-sabotage derives from a lack of self-worth. One way to build up your self-worth is to start believing in yourself and taking a chance on yourself. You must believe in yourself before others can. Be *okay* with rejection. Become desensitized to rejection; once you do this, there are no limits to what you can accomplish.

If you continue to engage in self-sabotage, you are subjecting yourself to an amply limited life. Do you want to continue blowing opportunities? Do you want to continue settling for mediocrity?

I had a close friend I was referring for a position at a top tech company I worked for, and they conveyed they felt out of their league; my friend

was acclimated to working for mediocre companies. I encouraged my friend to treat this new career opportunity just like any other opportunity and believe they have every right to be here.

Get comfortable with the uncomfortable. Realize that you don't have to continue settling for mediocre—this is a choice you can alter at any point.

<u>Put Yourself Out There: Here's Some Motivation</u>

Don't think you deserve the job? Apply for it anyway.

Don't think your article is good enough? Publish it anyway.

Don't think they'll reply to your email? Send it anyway.

Don't think they'll respond to your text? Send it anyway.

Don't think your picture is good enough? Post it anyway.

Don't think they'll accept you? Be yourself anyway.

Don't think you'll make the sale? Go for the sale anyway.

Don't think they'll go on a date with you? Ask to go out anyway.

Don't think you'll have enough strength to finish? Keep going anyway.

Don't think you can do it? Do it anyway.

Don't think you're young enough? Who cares.

Don't think you're attractive enough? So what?

Don't think you're beautiful? Be the new standard of beauty.

Don't think you're good enough? Go for it anyway.

Don't think you're healthy enough? Get healthy!

Don't think you're worthy enough? Fake it until you feel worthy enough.

Don't think they'll like you? Like yourself.

Don't think you're the right fit? Be the **new** fit.

Rejection Is Just Redirection

And when we put ourselves out there, we don't need to fear rejection. We can *embrace rejection*, knowing that we have a beautiful gift called self-acceptance. The right people and opportunities will accept us at the right time. Know that when you are rejected, you are merely being redirected in a better direction.

Closing Thoughts

Believe in yourself—even when you don't feel like it, or you feel you don't have the capability to believe. *Accept yourself*—even when you don't feel you're worthy of being accepted. Stop assassinating your opportunities! **Don't self-reject.**

Which one will be you?

Question

Do I accept and believe in myself?

_____

_____

_____

_____

_____

Notes Section

Article 7

Strict Parenting Taught Me NOT To Have Boundaries

It was not okay for me to have my own identity

Anyone deep into the self-help and personal development game knows that boundaries are pivotal to leading a successful, peaceful, and manageable lifestyle. (*Side Note: If you struggle with implementing boundaries and you haven't read "When to Say Yes, How to Say No To Take Control of Your Life" By Dr. Henry Cloud, get the book today.*) But let's keep it real here, many people struggle when it comes to boundaries.

What Do Firm Boundaries Look Like

One of my close friends has **firm** boundaries— unlike anyone I've met before, and it's not offensive *at all!* Boundaries are a natural aspect of who she is because she was taught from the beginning that it is *okay* to have them. She easily tells you if something is not okay with her. She will politely but (mostly) assertively convey to someone, who tries to interrupt her workout with a meaningless conversation, that she is getting back to her training—effective **immediately**.

We were roommates in college, and she has a garrulous nature. Whenever she was in her talking mood (which was most nights), I felt 100% comfortable telling her, "Hey, you're talking too much," and she accepted it easily, happily, and went on her merry way.

She has been a teacher to me for implementing boundaries into my life. I found her family life fascinating because I knew the cause of her boundaries was because her parents let her know it was okay to:

1. Voice her opinions without consequence.
2. Express her feelings and emotions—even if they differed from her parents.
3. Be who she is—unapologetically.

It's Starts In Childhood

You either have boundaries, or you don't, and it starts in childhood. Parents are usually the ones that teach them to you by example and how they raise you. Parents are the ones that let you know if your boundaries are okay to implement.

As kids, we naturally have boundaries from the beginning—if we don't experience too much trauma, too soon. It's normal for a kid to tell you if they don't like something, if they don't want to do something, if something doesn't feel right, if they don't like someone, if they don't want to go off somewhere with someone, etc. Kids are honest when they haven't been tainted too much by life and people.

Why Strict Parenting Can Eat Away Your Boundaries

My parents and I have an excellent relationship today, and we talk almost every day. Growing up, though, was an interesting story. My parents were amply strict—unnecessarily, I might add (I mean, I was the GOOD child #baffled). It was their way or the highway. There was no arguing, and if you did (like I did), it meant repercussions would ensue. It was not okay for me to state my opinion. It was not okay for me to say no. It was not okay for me to reject a hug I did not want from my family or people outside of my family. It was not okay for me to say I did not want to be a part of family movie night. **It was not okay for me to have my own identity.** All of this scarred me and hindered my development for healthy boundaries. *(Side Note: Aside from boundaries, there were many things my parents did **right.**)*

Generational BS

Looking back, I understand why my parents were the way they were (because of their own childhood trauma). If your parents don't have good boundaries, their parents didn't either. It's a generational effect that does not cease until

someone gets into enough pain to say,
"ENOUGH IS ENOUGH!" I got to this point but
still struggle with boundaries to this day in some
ways. But I am a lot better than I used to be.

A Letter to Parents

I'm calling out parents now...

Many issues that kids experience and face today
(drug addictions, having babies way too early,
dropping out of school way too early,
anorexia/bulimia, struggling with suicide, getting
bullied (in-person and digitally), getting into debt
way too early, etc.), well *some* of these issues are
because kids are taught:

- Who they are does not matter.
- What they say, think, and feel does not matter.
- Their identity is not invaluable.
- Having boundaries and saying "no" is not *polite* or okay.
- Being *different* is not okay.

- Following the crowd is the right thing to do.

I remember a story about a girl who struggled with anorexia because she felt forced to be a doctor because everyone in her family was a doctor. No one in the family had any identity other than a doctor. There were no boundaries, separate identities, or differing opinions. No one had their own voice or desires; they simply all did the same thing. She never understood why she developed the bizarre reaction (anorexia), but this was her way of coping with a lack of boundaries all her life.

Do Better

Parents need to do better. I know it's not easy, which is why I have not signed up for the job, but I was a kid once, and I know how it feels to have parents that don't allow you to have your own identity. I know how it feels to want to say "no" but instead learn to say nothing. I know how it feels to be angry because you're not *allowed* to have boundaries. I know how it feels to not be able to express your anger. I know how it feels to be silenced. I know how it feels to be diminished because your boundaries are not respected. I know how it feels to not be allowed to be yourself.

Don't Talk Back = Don't Have An Opinion/Be Silent

The whole "Don't talk back to me" thing that parents say to their children should be re-worded to something like:

- "I value your opinion—even if it's different than mine."
- "I would like to hear what you have to say—respectfully."

Don't silence your kids, or you are teaching them to be silent in the world. Kids' voices matter. Our voices matter. Who we are matters. Having boundaries matters. If you don't have boundaries, you will never live your life; you will always be subject to the whims of everyone around you. Without boundaries, you will never be the driver or in charge of your life. So, if you weren't taught boundaries growing up, this is the perfect time to start. It won't be easy, but it will be 100% worth it.

Question

If I am a parent, how can I ensure my kids develop strong boundaries? If I'm not a parent, and struggle with boundaries, what will I do from here to develop boundaries?

Notes Section

The End

Thank You Note

Thank you for taking the time to read this book, and I appreciate the opportunity you have given me to invest in your life.

About Destiny S. Harris

Destiny S. Harris' ultimate goal is to positively inspire, cultivate, elevate, and educate the minds of individuals across the globe through her writing and fit lifestyle.

With over 300+ books published to date, creating (whether it is books, articles, poetry, or music) has always been Destiny's thing, not to mention health & fitness and all things entrepreneurial. Destiny published her first book, "Beauty Secrets for Girls," at age 11, and her second book, "Don't Wait Until It's Too Late," at age 12.

Destiny obtained three degrees from the University of Georgia in Psychology, Political Science, & Cultural Studies. She also started her own music teaching business at the age of 14, which she led for over ten years. In addition, she has been teaching academic, career, and personal development topics to thousands of students and readers since 2004.

Outside of writing, Destiny loves and enjoys a few other things: bodybuilding, reading, traveling, dogs, food, classic movies, anime, mountain and ocean views, plants, and nature.

Check out her work, leave a review, share your thoughts with your friends and family, and be a part of a movement: helping people learn and grow through means of self-education (books).

Get Your Free Books @ Destinyh.com

<u>Or Complete the Following:</u>

Step 1: Go to <u>amazon.com/author/destinyharris</u>

Step 2: Filter Books By "Price: Low to High"

Step 3: Download any & all available free books

Connect W/ Destiny S. Harris

Please reach out and stay in touch. Destiny S. Harris enjoys chatting with readers. Start a conversation today.

Community

Web: destinyh.com

Blog: destinyharris.substack.com

Facebook: facebook.com/textdestiny

Instagram: instagram.com/textdestiny

Leave A Review

My goal is to positively impact as many lives across the globe as possible through my writing, and I need your help doing this. One way you can help me is to leave a book review, which will continue to help spread the word about my books.

When you have a moment, please take the time to review this book. Thank you in advance!

Share This Read

If you found this book valuable, please take the time to invest in someone else's life, share what you learned from this book, or loan your copy. It's good to give. It feels remarkable to give, and we mustn't keep all the good stuff to ourselves.

When You're Feeling Series

1. When You're Feeling Depressed

2. When You're Feeling Lonely

3. When You're Feeling Like Sh*t

4. When You're Feeling Afraid

5. When You're Feeling Discouraged

6. When You're Feeling Broke

7. When You're Feeling Impoverished

8. When You're Feeling Unmotivated

9. When You're Feeling Discontent

10. When You're Feeling Sick

11. When You Feel Like Quitting

12. When You're Feeling Insecure

13. When You're Feeling Lazy

14. When You're Feeling Tired

15. When You're Feeling Stressed

16. When You're Feeling Unhealthy

17. When You're Feeling A Loss of Identity

18. When You're Feeling Rejected

19. When You're Feeling Like A Failure

20. When You're Feeling Unconfident

21. When You're Feeling Holiday Stress

22. When You're Feeling Transition

23. When You're Feeling Anxiety

24. When You're Feeling Stuck In The Past

25. When You're Feeling Ignored

26. When You're Feeling A Lack of Peace

27. When You're Feeling Ugly

28. When You're Feeling Grief

29. When You're Feeling Financial Stress

30. When You're Feeling Anger

31. When You're Feeling Distracted

32. When You're Feeling Embarrassed

33. When You're Feeling Anxious On The Job

34. When You're Feeling Stupid

35. When You're Feeling Heartbroken

Overcoming BS Series

1. Affirmations to Overcome Abuse

2. Affirmations to Help Overcome Obesity

3. Bye Bye Sugar: Get Rid of the Addiction

4. From Pain to Freedom: Overcoming Abuse

5. Overcoming Embarrassment, Anxiety, Fear & Failure

6. 6 Steps to Overcome Your Emotional Addiction to Sugar

7. Codependent Emotional Eaters

8. The Problem With Long-Term Therapy

9. Overcome Troubled Relationships

Mental Rescue Series

1. Affirmations For: Depression

2. My Emotional Journey: A Workbook

3. Dealing With The Monday Blues

4. 31 Days of Encouragement for the Soul

5. 100 Ways To Improve Your Mood

6. Dealing With Loneliness

7. Escape The Drought

8. 30 Days of Relaxation

Self-Care Affirmations Series

1. Affirmations On Self-Care

2. Affirmations On Self-Care: Travel Size

Good Day, Good Night Series

1. Good Morning: Affirmations

2. Good Night: Affirmations

Boost Your Self-Esteem Series

1. Self-Boosting Affirmations

2. Affirmations For Approval Addicts

3. Self-Worth Affirmations

4. Self-Love Affirmations

5. Over 100 Ways To Feel Good

6. Affirmations: Be Fearless (Lightning Edition)

7. Believe In Yourself: Affirmations

The Law of Attraction Series

1. The Law of Attraction: Create Your Life

2. The Law of Attraction: Affirmations

3. Create Your Life: Write It Down

4. Think & Earn Six Figures

Level 1: Finance Series

1. Level 1: Finance for Students

2. Level 1: Finance for Women

3. Level 1: Finance Under 30

Building Wealth Series

1. Prosperity Affirmations
2. Wealth Affirmations
3. Money Affirmations
4. LOA Affirmations
5. Milk & Honey Affirmations

Post-Incarceration Series

Destiny S. Harris created the Post-Incarceration Series to give back to those affected by the correctional system. If you would like to support an inmate, please purchase one or more of the books below for an inmate you know or donate at paypal.me/supportdestiny to get one or more books delivered to an inmate.

Post-Incarceration Series

1. An Inspirational Love Letter To The Incarcerated
2. Boost Yourself: Affirmations
3. Go For Your Dreams
4. I Believe In Myself: Affirmations
5. I Do The Hard Sh*T: YES I CAN!
6. Love Yourself: Affirmations
7. Self-Value Affirmations
8. Career Mentorship: Get The Guidance You Need

Free Gift

Get Your Free Books @ Destinyh.com !

Or Complete the Following:

Step 1: Go to amazon.com/author/destinyharris

Step 2: Filter Books By "Price: Low to High"

Step 3: Download any & all available free books

Leave A Review!